To Sophie
Hope to
&

Maggie

LIPSTICK

Maggie Butt

GREENWICH EXCHANGE
LONDON

Greenwich Exchange, London

LIPSTICK
© Maggie Butt

First published in 2007
All rights reserved

Printed and bound by Q3 Digital/Litho, Loughborough
Tel: 01509 213456
Typesetting and layout by Albion Associates, London
Tel: 020 8852 4646
Cover design by Chance & Fat, London
Tel: 020 7490 5778

Cataloguing in Publication Data is available from the British Library.

Greenwich Exchange Website: www.greenex.co.uk

ISBN: 978-1-871551-94-5
ISBN: 1-871551-94-3

for my family

Acknowledgements

Some of these poems (or versions of them) have appeared in the following magazines:
Acumen, Agenda, Envoi, Equinox, How Do I Love Thee, Manifold, Obsessed with Pipework, Orbis, Other Poetry, Poems in the Waiting Room, Poetry Life, Poetry Salzburg, Quattrocento, Scintilla, Seam, Smiths Knoll, Snakeskin (homepages.nildram.co.uk), *South, The London Magazine, The Shop, Yellow Crane.*

'On My 85th Birthday' was the 18th Poetry Life competition winner judged by Ruth Padel; 'Kamikaze', 'Banana', and 'Initiation' were awarded prizes by the Writers Inc., the Essex and the Barnet poetry competitions respectively; the winter months of 'Calendar' appeared in *Winter Gifts*, (Happenstance Press, 2005); 'Chipko – 1978' appeared in *Images of Women*, (Arrowhead Press, in association with Second Light, 2006); 'Royal Vintage' is a 'poetry pf' Christmas card; 'Bulbs' and 'May' appeared in *Poems in the Waiting Room 1998 – 2006* anthology, and 'Bulbs' also appeared in *Poetry in Stitches*, (National Needlework Archive 2005), and was read by Imogen Stubbs on *Poetry Please*, (BBC Radio 4, February 2003).

Grateful thanks to Patricia Oxley for publishing my first pamphlet, *Quintana Roo*, in 2003, which included some of these poems. Thanks to June Hall for her clear critical eye and supportive comments.

Contents

Stonemason

I carve a head, shaping a nostril for breath,
though nobody will see it, high above the nave.
I am uncomfortable and scared of heights
but careful in each chisel-chip
tongue caught between my teeth.

The rising arcs of this steep-vaulted roof
soar high as youth's ambition.
Then I'd had hopes of forming an apostle
to look clear over rooves from the West front
admired from the cathedral close.

Now I'm content to find the faces in the stone:
a girl I loved but never dared to tell;
this gargoyle fashioned like my enemy;
a green man winking from his mask of oak
eyes crinkled with my father's laugh.

Chipko – 1978

We set off singing and with drums
close together in the pre-dawn grey
summon courage on the winding path.

Our feet talk to the dry cracked earth
where other trees once stood. Dust
blows determination in our eyes and mouths.

I lay my cheek against the knobbly bark
wrap arms around its years of growth
listen to sap rising, leaf-speak, green,

try not to see Amrita Devi, axed down
with her arms about a tree. My small heart
set against the strength of money.

The loggers are felled to silence at the sight:
bright saris flower against each dark trunk;
the forest, a garden of women.

Chipko roughly translates as 'tree hugging.' This movement saved a Himalayan
forest from being cut down for tennis rackets.

Morning Sunlight 1952

Edward Hopper

A rented bed in a rented room
far from the life I invented round myself
familiar cups, coughs, cushions,
air chewable with unspoken words
the plaintive *if* ... and *when* ...

I have slept in my sun-dress
colour of salmon / mouths / ripe flesh
woken before street sweeper time
by unaccustomed silence and the
mattress ghosts of stranger's bodies.

I sit for the stark greeting of this new-world light
bright glare of no hiding place.
My own shadow licks the bed
between my thighs, and dents the single pillow.
The sun soaks in and spreads like fingers down my veins.

Out of the window, a long straight road
of eyeless brownstone tenements
reminds me of the track along the sandspit
straight as sunlight, lapped with blue
far from the imposition of brick and glass.

But I shrug off the old skin of the past,
smooth out the dimpled hollow
where my feet rest on the rented sheet.
Life will resume, like the cranking up
of a newsreel in an old movie theatre.

Girl Power

Fierce currents round my life
have dragged my feet and carried me
oceans away from my safe mooring
flotsam on adult tides.

But look! Now I have power –
something which lies within my sole control.
I can close my lips and make
fat vanish magically from thighs and hips.
I lie in bed, discovering new bones
which I have made appear, fingering
the purity of their hollow whiteness.

I can make the scales say less each day
I can send my periods away
I can make myself so insubstantial,
that now I have the power to go or stay.

Fish Wife

Nae weddit tae the fish at a'
but impregnated, bonely-deep.

Five thoosan lassies track the fleet
a flock o seagulls followin the boats

hatit by low-season Southron landladies
wha tak oor fee but strip the rooms

fer fear fish-stench'd spoil guid furniture
wurmin, boring intae wood and cloth.

Ma riddened honds are intimate wi scales
an gills, roond staring een an guts

fingers numb, ower cauld tae feel
the lacerations o shairp needle banes.

Nae ither wurk sae carried like a stain
untouchables in kirk, in shop, in luve:

the reek o herrin wad imprint itsel
ontae the luver's pillow, settin' us apairt.

Smokin stink is woven tae the fibres
o ma duds, the lacin o ma flesh

ma hair is sea-weed, skin is brine
ma sisters rise in phosphorescent shoals.

Many thousands of Scots girls followed the herring fleet each year around the coast of Scotland all the way down to East Anglia.

Blind Date

i.m. Jean Paul. Her story.

Who could guess a blind-date dare would
lift me like a wave in Surrey
wash me to the Wolastoquik
where the woods dip to the river?
Old canoe now rocks beneath me
unreal as a waking dream,
all because I kissed a soldier
wore his nylons, ate his chocolate
staunched the wound of loneliness.
War and love split lives like lightening:
sisters weeping at the quayside,
me adrift upon a river,
with a priest my sole companion
who can translate into English,
gliding up-stream to my husband
with the child he's yet to hold.

Forty thousand brides on cruise ships
twenty thousand cooped-up kids,
waved off on a great adventure
high heels and our home made trousseaus
secret stash of favourite lipstick
snap shots of our mums and dads.
Canada is blue horizons
distances which swallow England;
brides now stand alone on prairies
weep for streetlamps, corner shops
feather beds and indoor lavvies
friendly neighbours who will listen
troubles halved and halved again;
most have no-one else to talk to
but the quiet stranger-husband
or the toddler in the cot.

Even on the Aquitania
I felt different from the rest.
Was it part of the attraction
half the thrill of saying *yes*
knowing I would be the only
white girl on the reservation,
not another no-one, nothing
shuffling in the rush-hour crowd?
Two years since our war-poor wedding –
seventeen seemed old enough if
he was old enough to fight.
Now the terror of my promise
overtakes me on the river,
weeks of travel tell me surely
as the silent brave who paddles –
all is left behind for ever.

How a moment rocks the future:
fingers touching in the darkness
of a smoky crowded dance hall
swept me from home counties life
to a world of smooth-backed rivers
trains and roads dissolved in silence
pine trees pierce the cloud-wide sky.
Canoe, river, dance hall fever
threads between old life and new.
Silver droplets glint the paddle
tree-clothed river banks assure me
as canoe prow parts the water
wake of yesterday behind us
all tomorrows lie in mist.
Blind-date, blind-faith, blind-love, blindfold
gliding into the unguessed.

Hijab

If it would help, think of me like a nun
who loves God more than glamour
makes your street her convent
clothes herself in prayer.

My dress caricatures me in your eyes
like stripey sweater and a bag of swag
the cowboy with the black hat/evil heart
as if Kalashnikovs clank round my knees.

Your barbed stares try to penetrate,
a blacked-out price on market goods,
trying to fool you with my foreign ways.
Or else you pity me, caged in cloth
and tamed by some fanatic ring-master.

But I reflect your pity-arrows back
bare-midriffed in your desperate race
to snare a man; outshine, outflash,
outburn, stay ever young. Exposed,
shame-stripped, you sell yourself too cheap.

You dance to some hypnotic global tune
twitch like puppets: starve, slice skin
thinner, younger, Barbie's acolytes.

While, quiet in my habit, I can be
exactly who I am.

Graduation

Faked pomp, fanfare and procession,
solemn cap-and-gown masquerade,
pretended lineage.
Students stacked high in rows,
like cans on supermarket shelves
waiting in purgatory to be called.
Flamboyant body art tidied away
uniformly tamed by academic gowns
EEC stamped, sized and graded
as graduating sausages.

But at the edge of the dais
where most pray not to trip
or nervously finger wobbly mortar board,
one tall black girl theatrically casts off her gown
and underneath a tight black leather mini-dress
is sprayed onto her body.
She strides onto the stage, ignoring dignitaries,
– a hush – anticipation – stewards tense –
she raises up long arms and parts her feet
stamping a great black X against the academics
and slowly executes two perfect cartwheels
across the space where others nod obsequiously
arm and leg spokes suspended in the air
a V to the establishment
a V for victory.

Jumble Sale

Poised for the opening, on guard behind
teetering piles of shirts and skirts,
boil-washed woollens, felted and shrunk.

Once coveted, saved for, bought,
matched with shoes and lipstick,
admired, dry-cleaned, hung carefully.

Clothes for promotion – for getting on.
Clothes for seduction – for taking off.
I loved you in that blue.

Hope pressed into them.
Longing nestled into fabric folds.
Anticipation waiting in the drawer.

And now the eager scramble for the best,
surging against trestle tables
jackdaw eyeing of another's find;

like writers rummaging the ragbag
of the world for words to buff up,
change the buttons, dress anew.

Dust films our fingertips and sets off sneezes
dead skin cells blizzarding the sunbeams
air riddled with the particles of past.

Nylon Sheets

This was the future come to pass
test-tube fibres, grown by science

housekeeping purses flew wide
as mouths of hungry baby birds

two pairs for each bed (one in the wash)
Buy British, dream smug in Bri-nylon

bedtime flashed and sparked in pink and mauve
designed by hippies on a psychedelic trip

thus swinging sixties cured the washday blues
no more heaving sodden cotton sheets

between the steamy twin-tub drums
these flew like fledglings, chirruping

replaced the sombre sails along the washing line
with gaudy parakeets, Carnaby Street carnival

dry in a trice and best of all, no ironing
(faint smell of charred bras carried on the wind.)

How did our mothers spend that newly minted time
which made it worth the sweaty, suffocating sleep

the slippery touch, the catching on rough heels
a generation rising charged with static?

Initiation

St Pancras Station, early Saturday,
clean and swept, airy as intention.

A fat man in a football shirt,
nylon, stripes of blue and white,
fit for a boat race, or a summer sky,
which stretches over cultivated belly
pregnant with beer and single mindedness.

(If he were sliced as thin as pepperami
each slice would bear his team's name
flourishing, gothic script, like a stick of rock.)

A small boy, skinny and baby-blonde,
swings on the railings, upside down,
dressed in the same sky strip, but in the genes
a slowly incubating photocopy of his dad.

The tiger's stripes are not just on his fur
but on the skin beneath.

Dad stops a passer-by and threateningly
menacing as a knife in a dark alley
thrusts out a cheap disposable camera
lines up beside his son, pats down his hair
and grins with pride, a pork-pie smile.

A dream fulfilled – *me and my boy* –
his first match, great initiation
into the soaring hope and dark despair
it means to be a man.

Heathrow? Heathrow?

Sometimes the contours of a stranger's face
imprint themselves, as though they map my life,
reveal coordinates of wider mysteries.

My tube pulls in to Leicester Square and through the glass
I watch a silent film: a rabbi on the packed platform
unseen to everyone but me, holds up a scrap of paper,
carefully copied letters in a foreign tongue;
mouths his English mantra *Heathrow? Heathrow?*
as though invoking secret names of God.

People surge around him like a tide. He a pebble,
buffeted on the beach, irrelevant to the hugeness of the ocean.
This isn't prejudice. This is its guilty twin, indifference.
He, lonelier than a man adrift upon the sea,
knowing his insignificance under the sweeping span of stars.
Heathrow? Heathrow? the futile prayer of waves upon a shore.

He is beyond my reach, beyond the carriage-glass
his battered suitcase at his feet, his hat, his curls,
his wiry beard, the paper talisman which he, a scholar,
has relied on. Words are his trade, his sanctuary, as mine,
our only chart to navigate these deeps.
Heathrow? Heathrow? will steer us home.

Halloween on the Piccadilly Line

The underground girls are bold with lager,
dressed to kill: fishnets, black lips, piercings,
spiders' webs etched on whitened skin;
they ride the rails to trick or treat.

"Parrots Settle in the Suburbs"

An emerald flock flashes out
lassoes the rooves of London
imported spice from paradise
flavour of dubloon, lagoon;
close to the airport, escapologists
multiplying in the wing-wide air.
No notion yet if they will turn
grey squirrel, knot-weed, mink
or if their tropic lime will blend
with cricket pitch and oak
viridian and verdigris
forest groves of Arden, Sherwood,
chord a bright note of light
in all the greens of England.

Up to 20,000 parrots are now living wild in London and the South East.
(BBC News Education)

e-mail

The thrill at first of messages from air,
a screen alive with busy conversation
the ego subtly flattered.

Until the junk mail blossomed like a fungus
a daily chore of skimming off the scum
to find the meaty-matter.

Too many people with too much to say
all day, all night, all round the globe
the electronic chatter.

This must be what it's like for God.
"You have six billion unread messages."

He isn't dead; he's just logged off
and gone out for a stroll
through whorling galaxies
of less demanding stars.

X-Rays

Roll up, roll up to see the bones
Yer livin' skelington!

They queued in summer's fainting heat
stiff collars and tight corsets wet with sweat
odour of bodies trained for Empire's sacrifice.
(The barker's family stricken with a sickness
caused by defying nature.)

Those rays which cut through crinolines
displayed the clear shape at the core,
a monkey puzzle tree of bones,
but failed to clue the outline of the soul
or solve the mystery of its whereabouts.

Frock-coated young gents hoped to spy
beneath the laced-up layers of their sweethearts' clothes.
Plump flesh eluded them, the rays sliced far too deep,
they glimpsed instead the grim memento mori –
all that remains of beauty and of love.

They turned aside to soft shale of the cliffs
to imprints of fish, trilobites, ammonites
where the rock had x-rayed them
and filed away for future reverence
amazement at these once teeming oceans.

Now those young men and women too
are stripped to bone, impressed upon the mud
divest even of the modesty of coffins,
petrifying under weight of time
as if the x-rays told the only truth.

Spaces

Huge crimson doors flung wide
shameless as a strip-tease
reveal a cavernous space
empty of fire engines,
and four black lace-up shoes tossed
higgledy-piggledy on the concrete
smelling of socks and haste.
Shouts and running trembled
to silence in the exhaled air.

So it must be in war-time when
young pilots scramble to the skies
leaving half-drunk tea, a bitten sandwich,
a hangar, ballroom-vast and lofty,
echoing with the age-old
adrenalin of going into battle.

But there are greater spaces still
recently vacated, large as light
palpable and noisome
wind eddying in the rafters,
and clues to read them:
spectacles sightless on the hall table
a book, face down, wordless, by the bed.

History Tin

Mum's button tin was round as years,
purpled with pansies, an open-sesame
of dazzle, sorted on the kitchen table
like forty greedy thieves. A treasure trove

which whispered childhood in the slump,
a world where hunger slouched in doorways
or flu snatched young men from their clothes
where ornament came small and circular.

Mum's button tin held her world war
carved quiet in black bakelite,
and older, pearlised, horn and jet
cut from rag-thin frocks of grandmothers

whose lives were darned by gas-light
raising sons to fuel the great machines
of war, buttoning their great-coats
to walk the long walk out of sight.

War Cry

Those old words slime again from the sewers
drag themselves erect, clothed in shining apparel
as though they descend from holy places,
form up in drill-ranked sentences
brandishing swords of justice:
Follow me into battle.

Behind the burnished copper shields of rhetoric
march ranks of boys with faces burned away
mothers with their hearts clawed from their bodies
ghost babies never to be conceived.

Small

Let me be a lone mosquito hunting
in the dark, dive bombing into ears,
stealing sleep, carrying fatal charge.

Let me be a hair-line fracture in the slim
bone of a toe, shifting stride to shuffle
tumbling the proud edifice of the body.

Let me be a Lisbon flower girl
who slips a fresh carnation in the barrel
of a gun, and blooms a revolution.

Lipstick

In wartime women turn to red
swivel-up scarlet and carmine
not in solidarity with spilt blood
but as a badge of beating hearts.

This crimson is the shade of poets
silenced for speaking against torture,
this vermilion is art
surviving solitary confinement,

this cerise defies the falling bombs
the snipers taking aim at bread-queues,
this ruby's the resilience of girls
who tango in the pale-lipped face of death.

War photographer, Jenny Matthews, noticed that in Bosnia and Afghanistan
women favoured bright red lipstick. Max Factor confirm the same was true
during the Second World War.

PoW

Freighted from Egypt, inching in truckloads
up the hot leg of Italy, caged homing birds
northing by date-palm, vineyard, edelweiss.

One thought churns the miles, strange syllables
formed by teeth and lips, the unfamiliar hum
of home-words: beit, casa, heimat.

A London boy, sure-footed in alleys and yards,
surveys the rearing mountains, coifed chalets
cauldrons of cloud around the peaks

firs with winter tangled in their branches,
plans spring escape: a hike to Switzerland,
like crossing Piccadilly blindfold.

Compass needle swings to that bombed out
house in Hoxton, true magnetic north
hours turning and turning it closer.

Kamikaze

(Found poem)

You have lived for 20 years or more.
You feel that you are floating in the air.
Breathe deeply three times. Then you are no more.

Transcend life and death. Spirit and skill are one.
Totally disregard your earthly life.
You have lived for 20 years or more.

Prepare well your inner self. Harmonise your height.
Do not waste your life lightly. Do your best.
Breathe deeply three times. Then you are no more.

A loyal fighting man is a pure-hearted filial son.
You see your mother's face. It is her usual face.
You have lived for 20 years or more.

Speed has increased by a few thousand-fold.
The spirits of your dead comrades are watching you.
Breathe deeply three times. Then you are no more.

You may hear a final sound like the breaking of crystal.
All the cherry blossoms will smile brightly at you.
You have lived for 20 years or more.
Breathe deeply three times. Then you are no more.

Lines from *Kamikaze Pilot's Manual*, tr. Albert Axell.

7, 8, 9

7/7
The clacking of the rails is premonition
like the chatter of angry starlings

low whine in the distance of a barely felt
anxiety about the possibility of pain

hot rush of air lifts strands of hair
approach sweeping away doubt

white lights appearing in the tunnel
are the eyes of the angel of death

the squealing redgrey dragon
arrives to speed you into night

8/7
My empty train crawls through King's Cross
pauses for a heart-beat at the deserted platform.
Ghost faces peer into my carriage, clamouring
for seats, try to prise the door.
I cannot meet their eyes. Dip my head.

9/7
The conference hall hums like a hive.
We gather in our noise, rounding it up
like naughty children or a huge dog
on a leash. A thousand voices
movements hushed, our thoughts rise
as smoke and gather in the rare, still air.
Silence is all we have to offer.

Allotments

Untended, bramble thickets scale the trees,
lawless flutter-hearted hunting ground
dense thorny undergrowth where fox is king,
and fruit, once gathered in for jams and pies
falls to the ground, replenishes the earth.

They were the pulse of England once
a constant heart, drumming steady time;
creosoted potting sheds, hoed rows
splashed pink-and-green with apple blossom
the steadfast thump of boot on fork.

War-fractured soldiers dug away the pain
seed beds their regeneration in the silence
of no-guns. Rich earth repaid hard work with bounty,
nightmares buried as the shoot became a meal
home-coming bike piled with fresh vegetables.

Last urban men to give thanks for the harvest
blue rows of cabbages, plump and ready to unfold
wigwam of jaunty red flowers magic into beans
painstaking alchemy of manure to feast,
blackberry stain evidence of a day well spent.

Hardship produced lush fruitfulness
cloches glinted in the pools of sunlight
rhubarb leaf umbrellas, humped potato rows
smells of soil and sweat and satisfaction
armfuls of dahlias offered to the shrine of peace.

Miracle at the Wedding in Taunton

They hook their sticks over the chair-back;
white haired, man and wife for fifty years,
yet as they touch the dance-floor

she takes his hand and lightens on her feet
years and sorrows fall away like a discarded dress
stepped out of, kicked aside, crumpled on the floor.

Pain lifts its veil, rain clears across the hills,
as though some merciful monarch sent a messenger
rushing in with a reprieve from age,

as if it were possible to rewind like a video
and find a different story, dance this time
to a different tune.

Technology

We have waved our hands
over the silence of parting
and conjured voices.

We have blinked at hours
of trudgery, and purred miles
under wheels and wings.

We have heard teeth chatter
in dark, fired up the night
blazed warmth into bones.

We have breathed into still lungs,
beatless hearts, empty wombs
and waked them, morning.

On my 85th Birthday

For breakfast there will be chocolate,
heaped and glossy like a race-horse,
sweating with saturated fat.

And I will devour it,
cramming in the melting mouthfuls
coating my fingers and my face.

In the morning I'll ride a motorbike
black leathers and no helmet
white hair streaming loose, a challenge.

For lunch there will be crispy bacon
in white bread, with butter,
mouthwatering aroma of defiance.

After my nap in the bed-shop window;
I will invite my doctor in for scones,
and lick thick clotted cream along the knife.

And in the sunset
I will ascend to heaven in a glider
singing in the eerie silence.

The next day I'll dance barefoot in the rain
or take up smoking (inhaling deeply)
or sub-aqua diving,
or run with scissors

if I choose.

Sunbathing

In between the clouds I will stretch out
listen to the leaves draw in its strength
absorb this solar energy, store it in my bones,
so when I'm pressed like dinosaur-age trees
when I am caught beneath the drudgery of time,
the weight of winter, I may spark into life
as coal in a welcome grate, returning the sun's fire.

Handkerchief

I drink the slope of fields
of stone walled cottages
small lambs, wired for bounce,
and wish I could fold up the countryside
and pocket it, to open on a sordid
city dawn, like a fresh linen handkerchief.

Star-lit

Laughing home barefoot from the disco
star-lit, care-free, safe within the pack
high heels dangling from our hands like bracelets,
cold pavements salve dance-blistered toes,
the pulse of living sings along our blood.
We are reflected in dark High Street windows
so the night is full of us, our youth.
The cars are few, our voices own the air,
and you three boys stride out, long-limbed,
the world laid out before you for the taking,
throw back your heads, cry to the moon,
We are gods!
And I look
And you are.

Ginger Beer

Days then were long with possibility
yeast and ginger scents of promise
bubbles rising with anticipation.
Summer played away.

Mysterious ginger beer plant
– beige gloop – no leaves or roots or branches.
Add water and divide to sentry bottles
parading in the side-way
tantalising as Lolita or forbidden chocolates
on a Christmas tree.

Now I rush it home before vanishment
handle with gloves, like nitroglycerine –
sip, silken cream but needles dancing on the tongue
freezing the temples / lingering bazaar glow.

One dawn we shocked awake
to cowboys firing guns outside the kitchen
and morning-wise the sad remains
bled away to sticky dregs and broken glass.

Banana

The banana on my desk
custard yellow, speckled brown
pockmarked as a Regency buck
or ancient liver-spotted hands
carries a sticker saying 'Windward Isles'
a triangle, blue/lemon with a palm tree
and for a moment my grey office
rings with the shouts of shirt-stripped men
labouring under an unforgiving sun
the shudder of a spider, withdrawing to the shadows
a swish and sigh as waves suck back the sand.

Royal Vintage

A court of princes froths from the school gate
each one is crowned, lord of delight,
in gold card, glitter gems, foil sapphires
clear as eyes. Fresh from nativity and tight
with cake and games and lemonade
they light the street's too-early night
bubbling, fermented, sun-drenched crop
fizz towards Christmas, bauble-bright.

Hand-held adults, wholly in their thrall
will store this vintage in the cellars of the mind
to uncork radiance when the prince is tall.

Apples

I know how apples should be stored:
wrapped singly in crumpled newsprint
laid side-by-side in neat geometry
their grid set in a cold dry airy place;

but in this fat and fertile land
oozing honey from its every pore,
I failed to set aside some richnesses
against the day when cold winds
slice through famine-flimsy clothes
and all this glistening sweetness is dried up;

instead I heaped my apples wantonly
a careless pile in our damp shed
and look how rot has spread
quiet as cancer through the crop.

I picture holding a fresh-picked russet
texture of woodland bark
curved to the curve of hands
smelling its spring-tang, teeth
overpowering the resistance of its flesh
the juices running on my tongue.

Elegies

Soft underfoot, walking on summer's pride
smell of fallen leaves, decay's shocking sweetness
a land of verticals, drawing the eye up
columns of temples from a world before temples,
solidity, despising man's short time-frame
slowing down our hurry, shutting for the winter
like shops in seaside towns; rain drips from leaf
to leaf long after the storm has passed.

Acorns, brown as the dying leaves
a whole tree in my hand, its branches
thick enough to wrap my arms around, to climb
riding the boughs windwards, creak of ship's timbers,
leaf-song urgent as the rush of water over weir,
rippling river, rustle of silk, turning of pages,
whispered elegies for the elms, answering and answering.

Calendar

I
January
Blackbird breaks the night
Pours liquid song in darkness
Auguring the dawn

XII
December
One pink rose
Clings to the leafless bush
Holds onto the past

II
February
Fish frozen in pond
Black ice, gold streaks, motionless
Practising for death

XI
November
A flurry of leaves
A darkness of mornings
A slip of pavements

III
March
Drowsy bumblebee
Lurching, drunk on sleep and sun
Wakes to a new world

X
October
Beech hedge camouflage
Olive, golden, copper
To battle winter

IV
April
Cars along the road
Plastered with pink polka-dots
Clowning Cherry trees

IX
September
Goldenest mornings
Glowing with false promise
Chill dusk tells the truth

V
May
Dark green leaves erect
In dank forgotten corners
White bells heaven scent

VIII
August
Heat clings to the skin
Urban feet seek dappled shade
Wasps scent a picnic

VI
June
Bees bounce on the chives
Nod down the pom-pom blooms
Greeting and farewell

VII
July
Purpled droplets fall
Sodden, chastened Buddleia
Clouds of forgiveness

Tumbling

The weeks are tumbling over one another
over and over like Chinese acrobats:
impossible handsprings, effortless,
tinsel-dressed, bright with sequins
spangles and greasepaint and sweat
somersaulting so fast they are blurred
until you can't see where one starts and
another finishes, tumbling out of the circus tent
on and on, up the dusty hillside road
off to the horizon.

Busybody

I thought time would slip in
under cover of night
a shadow stealthily stealing
away these precious hours,
but she comes in daylight
in full view of the neighbours
a busybody bailiff with a clipboard
resting on her copious bosom
to catalogue and label for removal
all that we hold dear.

Extras

A walk-on cast of thousands
swells the crowd scenes of my life,
hurrying to their other roles
as soon as my back is turned.
No green room or dusty wings
to rest between their takes,
removing make-up, yawning,
phoning agents, gossiping,
passing the time until my final act,
great denouement,
when they will purse their lips
and weep, then pack away their costumes
shrugging on cold air at the
stage door like an overcoat.

House-ghosts

The house shifts in its sleep
grumbles gently, snores and scratches;
small creatures run within its walls.

Nightsounds are amplified by darkness,
mysterious poundings of the heart of the house
clickings, clacketings of its internal working,

breath of its breathing, echoes of former occupants'
grief and lovemaking absorbed into its plaster
exhaled under cover of night.

Some of the ghosts have come along with me:
the fingers of a sinewed worker's hand,
which rub my back in comfort,

a girl's voice, singing far off
and unaware of listeners,
echoes in the dark.

The Holiday Brochure Didn't Show

Who would have thought
a water buffalo would gaze at me
and struggle up from his mud hip-bath
like an elderly cleaning lady from her knees
and raise his head to pose for my camera
against the paddy fields' eye-hurt green.

Who would have thought
that lizards, cocktail-bright and quick
which cling to wooden eaves with suction feet
would call and chatter to each other
like starlings or excited teenage girls
in the Ladies at a disco.

Who would have thought
a gaudy clown-fish would parade itself
and coral sway like washing on a line
while still as taxidermy on a sportsman's wall
a barracuda hangs immobilized
scowling behind his third-world dentistry.

Who would have thought
I'd let London pavements pound my soles
while somewhere on the other side of night
green lizards gossip on the ceilings
and silent barracuda eyes up lunch
as if I were a dream.

Quintana Roo

(i)
Driving though blizzards of butter-golden
butterflies. Mile after mile, hour after hour
veils of them ahead, bird-sized, iridescent blues
wings beating in distant applause,
cabbage-whites like pallid English tourists
populous as beach-wraiths.

Car-less roads stretching to tomorrow
straight as honesty, flanked by jungle
black hawks circling overhead.

No farm, no village, no peasant hut
but far ahead a butterfly-crowd
of bright-garbed Mayan Indians
clustered round a car crash
whole families on giant tricycles,
drawn, like the hawks, by death.

(ii)
Chichén Itzá, palace of panic
home of human sacrifice
a gruelling climb in slavering sun,
sheer edge which drops away
stairs only visible as you lean out
falling, always falling.

Inside the temple of terror,
no cooling labyrinth
but steps again, sweating slime
oozing walls, the exhaled breath
and fear of centuries,
falling, always falling.

Quintana Roo is a province of Mexico.

(iii)
The Plough carves a curious furrow
splitting the sky from breast-bone to pubis,
a pan, tip-toe on its handle-end.

The moon has turned her face away
from the glare of Venus, bright
as a floodlight on the horizon.

(iv)
Palm tree leaves
fingering the sky
playing scales
of light and shade

(v)
Garlanded with rifles, pistols, holsters,
soldiers lounge at the road-block,
impassive and deadly as the black hawks overhead,
peer into the car, eye the flawless flesh
of daughters in their shorts and strappy tops.
I wonder wildly if they would take me instead,
think of Boudicca weighing the odds
the grandchildren she'd never hold
mutely handing poison to her weeping girls.

(vi)
Mildew rejoices in the fetid air
spreading its dark infectious rash
insidious student-hovel smell
into wardrobes and corners.

(vii)

Resist the purple undertow
dragging, cajoling, tempting –
steady yourself, loose-limbed
time the onrush and push clear
the suck and hiss of surf –
lifted, carried in the white
rush of abandonment.

(viii)

Springy turf, smell of new-cut hay
low sun, now sorry for its burning noon
swallows swooping into the blind windows
of the abandoned bleached-white
Tulum temple complex, cliff-high
above the Caribbean, once a town
as populous as Seville.

Over each door a carving
inverted god, descending
wings folding, born head-first
into this earthly paradise.

Russian Tales

The film runs and I step into it, blinking
                against Baltic light, clear as a chorister's rising notes
but casting long, low shadows.
                     Russian dolls: a mystery within a mystery,
everything contrariwise as wonderland, and I am Alice.
                Cold burns the face, ice-drops my eyelashes,
frost sparkles the turrets of this Magic Kingdom.
                Snow falls: filmic dry flakes and polystyrene balls
and I in my every-day shoes.

The Russian heart frosted with hardship;
                small women wrapped in elegant fur coats
which swish and prowl, or stalk like bears
            or hang on mannequins, trapped in a glazed arcade
while I hear wraith-cries blowing from the gulags.

Within these alien churches, turban-topped,
                gold onion domes, criss-crossed with piety,
rise mosaic scenes from childhood Sunday-school
            of Jesus by the lake, familiar as bread and butter.
Heavy silver icons, the pauper Christ child
                peeps through ostentatious gilding;
so love can suffocate the thing it loves.

Scarlet carnations scattered on snow graves
                blood stains crystallised like sugared fruit,
Snow-white, Rose-red. Here fairytales take flesh;
            the wax-work Lenin in his gloomy mausoleum,
like Sleeping Beauty in glass coffin.

My train rolls slowly through these northern forests,
                snow quilts the steep-rooved houses,
which come and go through carriage windows;
                snow-drooped branches, silver knees in drifts,
sparkle in the spell of the Snow Queen.

We are sheltered in our plush compartment
                         as princesses in their boxes at the ballet
whose time has passed, their whistle blown,
                and I remember cattle trucks of human dreams
which rattled this way, into endless night.

Eternal flame leaps skywards in a deserted snow-bound park.

Revellers

And we are Venice now
water lapping our thresholds
bruising marble olive green
rusting feet of iron gates
reinventing our mythologies.

Our waking sounds are medieval,
handcarts trundled over cobbles;
dusk is a violin beneath a bridge;
lullabies the slap of waves on hulls
gondolas restless at their moorings.

Let us be masked revellers: defy
crumbling stucco, exposed brick,
mould stains' gloomy augurs;
dance away everpresent danger
skim the transparent mirrored water.

The Alchemist

He is intent, by slow degrees, on turning grief
to silence, walling it in blocks of ice
huge in each city centre, where folk
will point and marvel at its powerlessness.

On his small scales he measures out
a witches brew of gossips' tongues,
cat-calls, lovers' whispers, babies' wails,
girls' giggles, lost chords, feathered throats.

And soon enough his hoar-frost runnels creep
to offices and homes, paint fern-shapes
on the window panes, fractals on the mirrors.
Around the tea-table we turn our collars up,

stamp our feet against the soundless chill.
The clank of cutlery is muffled under snow
conversation lost in distance through the fog
voice boxes tissue-wrapped in frozen cloud.

He is tireless with the tools of transmutation.
I wait to see if alchemy is more effectual
than my attempt to transform sorrow's stone
to seas of salt, and tidal waves of tears.

Shadows

How blue the welcome shade
tossed lightly over shrivelled grass
by a lone desert tree; a shawl
crocheted from night
resting on my shoulders.

How strange that running water
throws a flowing image on the wall.
The unseen leaves an indentation
on the surface of the world;
aspens shudder from a touch
of angels' breath.

How long the sun-dial finger
cast by love
slowly arcing on the lawn
even when the sun has set.

Bright Fishes

Your struggle for life
was a man moving backwards
down the longest corridor
while his legs walked forwards.

Each drop of it precious
skittering away like mercury
bright fishes slipping through fingers
no net to hold them.

Canute against the tide
thin-lipped determination
will to bend iron
courage against knives, scalpel deep.

Set against this scalding memory
other news which reaches me –
simple slitting of wrists
and ebbing of blood.

Ice Rink

Four years.
And now the cavernous well
which yawned inside
has become so familiar
that I can skirt around
its slippery-scree edges
with confident, easy steps.

Slowly I have papered over
the beckoning blackness
(don't look down!)
with strips of translucent tissue paper;
building layer upon layer
into a papier mâché ice rink
crisp as an egg shell,
which one day
may be strong enough to bear my weight.

Fathering

Because I could not bear to let you go
my body found a way to bring you back.

Part-dormant genes pushed out a root
and half of me took flower.

My jowls drop just a feather's breadth
until your jaw-line smiles back from the mirror.

I swim the strokes you longed
and my slow breathing meets with yours.

You use my eyes to note the detail of the world
your calmness soothes my path like honey.

Because I could not bear to let you go
my body found a way to bring you back.

Bulbs

For a scientific daughter

I ask you – how the hibernating bulb
knows when to jerk awake?
Pinioned in the ice-dark earth
perpetual night of wet and cold
how does it know the time has come
to push the bleached blind maggoty shoot
out into the stone-frost dirt
on cue to flower on April 23rd?

I dare you – take a bulb and strip away
its glossy, coppery paper shell
the onion-like white folds on folds
and show me where it keeps the clock
or microchip which tells it when to start
so it will flower to the day with its companions
however chill and damp the spring.
One laggard never oversleeps and pops up in September.

I defy you – take the spiralling DNA of me
the pumping, wooshing ventricles,
the zing-charged porridge in my head,
and show me where I keep the love for you
that will outlast my life.

Stabiliser

I steady your first ride.
Fine-tuned to you from birth
the clearest station on the dial.
I wobble when you wobble.

Sometimes I spin in air
as you list left, lurch back
to crash land on my chest,
perpetual safety net.

Your confidence swells like a melon
watered by moonlight,
and on the curious machine of balance
hands click into alignment.

You soar, you glide, you race
free-fall parachutist, rushing wind
I barely tip the ground
a carried side-car passenger.

Now unscrewed, disengaged, I wait,
trying not to rust upon the garage shelf
in case your undreamed children need me.
But I still wobble when you wobble.

Gap Year

(i) Le Soir à la Fenêtre
Tangled in my underwater arms
drowning in seaweed green
you turn your head towards the open window
breathe deep draughts of cool lilac air,
ready yourself to dive into the road
which flows between our houses
curls away like a sea-serpent's tail
swallowed by night.

High in the blueberry sky
a purple-breasted phoenix
calls you to fly before the moon has waned,
for you are made of thistledown.
White puffs of smoke, left luminous in its wake
promise you even I will rise again
when you are fledged and flown.
A fresh new moon will slip its sliver
into the indigo dusk.

(ii) Embryo
Unhappiness curls in me
tight as a foetus
sucks its thumb and turns
an astronaut's slow somersault,
kicks a little, just to warn me.

It doesn't show yet
but I can hear it growing,
flexing its fingers
listening to the muffled world,
eyes wide open in the reddening gloom.

'Le Soir à la Fenêtre'
Marc Chagall, 1950

I wonder, like a schoolgirl with a secret,
how this monstrous birth
may be averted.

(iii) Travel Blues

You hear the song of distant dream-time places,
Long empty beaches echo in your eyes,
I dread the draw of those wide open spaces.

Your toes are itching, cheeks flush and pulse races,
Longing to go before youth's freedom flies,
You hear the song of distant dream-time places.

Long sands where noisy tourists leave no traces
Call you to launch yourself upon the skies;
I dread the draw of those wide open spaces.

The thrill of crowds with unfamiliar faces
Once stopped my youthful ears to parents' sighs,
I heard the song of distant dream-time places.

When everything you need's stuffed in two cases
I'll try to smile and wave at our good-byes,
I've felt the draw of those wide open spaces.

I'll count the days until our next embraces,
And wrap the world in your loved lullabies,
Soft hum the song of distant dream-time places,
To dance with you in those wide open spaces.

(iv) Demeter

When you tuck your daughter on the train
and watch her wan face slide into the night
and you are left upon the platform
with your tears, so small within your skin,
shrunk to a whisper as love pulls away;
you turn towards the tube's wide mouth
descending to the hot rebreathing air,
knowing how simple it would be
to ride the escalator into Hades' flames
if you had just a whisker of a chance
to bring her back with you.

(v) Parting

 No wonder the heart gives out in the end
throws up its hands and cries surrender
when it is stretched so many times in parting
like over-washed elastic.

(vi) Spotlight

Dispel my disbelief God,
focus your spotlight on the one
among those teeming masses,
pick her out, illuminate her path.

(vii) Coracle

I sew a sturdy coracle of words
woven with spells and caulked in luck,
speed it down rivers of night
to rock you in the lapping waves.

(viii) May

May doesn't give a damn about our squally nights
and overwork, and dusty city streets;

she sparks up candles on the chestnut trees
exuberant as Christmas in the suburbs,

spreads luminous bluebells and forget-me-nots
in dappled twilight underneath the trees,

allows the don't-care dandelions and celandines
to riot on grass verges with the daisies,

hangs cherry trees with bridesmaids' posies
painting the earth with petals, candy pink,

unfolds each ripe and bursting sticky bud
to fingers of fine-drawn lime leaves,

hides creamy mob-cap bells of lily of the valley
swirling their perfume in the shadowy nooks,

lets hawthorn snow-drift in the hedgerows,
unseasonable whiteness weighing down the boughs

soaks up the blackbird's song in elderflowers
hoarding its sweetness, ready to release in wine,

waves trees' defiant branch-loads at the clouds
to say, *We're still here. We survived the worst*

and oh, she hurls the purple scent of lilac and wisteria
onto the wind, summoning you home.

Mislaid

I am mislaid, lost luggage
in a warehouse of brown bags,

or one last case forever circulating
on the baggage reclaim belt.

I rummage through old photographs
scanning for my face I knew,

I search among the ashes of the fire
rooting like a boar for truffles;

but only find what I have lost
when I prepare to lose it once again in you.

Love Seeps In

Love seeps in and fills me up
as water overruns a sinking ship,
snaking down corridors
coating them with silver,
bubbling through cracks and crevices
thundering up staircases,
claiming everything.

Seven Ages of Love

1
sweet spurts of stupefaction
fountains of faithful milk
hard/soft nipple anchorage

2
toes curl around the tightrope
hands outstretched wide for balance
safety net of waiting arms

3
bones soften and liquefy
at the caught glimpse of your back
soft sweep of your whispered name

4
reckless leap of promises
over the edge of the cliff
gripping one-another's hands

5
the circle is completed
in that moment when you shield
their small body with your own

6
old friends, comforting slippers
worth far more than paid-up cheques
cash dividend of a life

7
silently it soaks away
as water poured onto sand
life itself loved best of all

Also published by Greenwich Exchange

Story: The Heart of the Matter **edited by Dr Maggie Butt**

What can't we get enough of: Food? Sex? Alcohol? Stories? We devour hundreds of stories every day in television news, magazines, fiction, gossip, movies, jokes, music videos, advertisements, plays, newspapers, and we never get tired of them. They leave us hungry for more.

This book examines how you can be a maker of great stories for a range of forms and media. The authors include novelists, journalists, poets, screenwriters, playwrights, a writer of short stories, a documentary maker, an oral storyteller and a stand-up comic, who offer personal insights into their art. Their examination of themselves as story makers sheds new light on what different forms, media and genres have in common, rather than what separates them. These entertaining and accessible essays are a must for teachers, students and practitioners of creative writing.

Contributors
Prof Graeme Harper, Portsmouth University, aka writer Brooke Biaz.
Prof Phillip Gross, University of Glamorgan, poet and children's writer.
Dr Mary Hammond, Open University, novelist and publishing history expert.
Prof Andrew Melrose, University of Winchester, children's writer and screenwriter.
Dr Neil McCaw, University of Winchester, director of the BA in Creative Writing.
Michelene Wandor, Royal Literary Fund fellow, playwright, poet, short story writer.
Dr Farah Mendlesohn, Middlesex University, science fiction expert.
Helena Nelson, teacher, poet and publisher.
Dr David Rain, Middlesex University, novelist.

Sarah Boston, Middlesex University, documentary film maker.
Sally Pomme Clayton, Middlesex University, oral storyteller.
Dr Sarah Niblock, Brunel University, journalist.
Russell Kane, stand up comic.
James Martin Charlton, Middlesex University, playwright and scriptwriter.

GREENWICH EXCHANGE BOOKS

POETRY

Adam's Thoughts in Winter *by Warren Hope*
Warren Hope's poems have appeared from time to time in a number of literary periodicals, pamphlets and anthologies on both sides of the Atlantic. They appeal to lovers of poetry everywhere. His poems are brief, clear, frequently lyrical, characterised by wit, but often distinguished by tenderness. The poems gathered in this first book-length collection counter the brutalising ethos of contemporary life, speaking of, and for, the virtues of modesty, honesty and gentleness in an individual, memorable way.
2000 • 46 pages • ISBN 978-1-871551-40-2

Baudelaire: Les Fleurs du Mal *Translated by F.W. Leakey*
Selected poems from *Les Fleurs du Mal* are translated with parallel French texts and are designed to be read with pleasure by readers who have no French as well as those who are practised in the French language.
F.W. Leakey was Professor of French in the University of London. As a scholar, critic and teacher he specialised in the work of Baudelaire for 50 years and published a number of books on the poet.
2001 • 152 pages • ISBN 978-1-871551-10-5

'The Last Blackbird' and other poems by Ralph Hodgson *edited and introduced by John Harding*
Ralph Hodgson (1871-1962) was a poet and illustrator whose most influential and enduring work appeared to great acclaim just prior to, and during, the First World War. His work is imbued with a spiritual passion for the beauty of creation and the mystery of existence. This new selection brings together, for the first time in 40 years, some of the most beautiful and powerful 'hymns to life' in the English language.
John Harding lives in London. He is a freelance writer and teacher and is Ralph Hodgson's biographer.
2004 • 70 pages • ISBN 978-871551-81-5

Lines from the Stone Age *by Sean Haldane*
Reviewing Sean Haldane's 1992 volume *Desire in Belfast*, Robert Nye wrote in *The Times* that "Haldane can be sure of his place among the English poets." This place is not yet a conspicuous one, mainly because his early volumes appeared in Canada, and because he has earned his living by other means than literature. Despite this, his poems have always had their circle

of readers. The 60 previously unpublished poems of *Lines from the Stone Age* – "lines of longing, terror, pride, lust and pain" – may widen this circle.
2000 • 52 pages • ISBN 978-1-871551-39-6

Martin Seymour-Smith – Collected Poems *edited by Peter Davies* (180pp)
To the general public Martin Seymour-Smith (1928-1998) is known as a distinguished literary biographer, notably of Robert Graves, Rudyard Kipling and Thomas Hardy. To such figures as John Dover Wilson, William Empson, Stephen Spender and Anthony Burgess, he was regarded as one of the most independently-minded scholars of his generation, through his pioneering critical edition of Shakespeare's *Sonnets*, and his magisterial *Guide to Modern World Literature*.
To his fellow poets, Graves, James Reeves, C.H. Sisson and Robert Nye – he was first and foremost a poet. As this collection demonstrates, at the centre of the poems is a passionate engagement with Man, his sexuality and his personal relationships.
2006 • 182 pages • ISBN 978-1-871551-47-1

Shakespeare's Sonnets *by Martin Seymour-Smith*
Martin Seymour-Smith's outstanding achievement lies in the field of literary biography and criticism. In 1963 he produced his comprehensive edition, in the old spelling, of *Shakespeare's Sonnets* (here revised and corrected by himself and Peter Davies in 1998). With its landmark introduction and its brilliant critical commentary on each sonnet, it was praised by William Empson and John Dover Wilson. Stephen Spender said of him "I greatly admire Martin Seymour-Smith for the independence of his views and the great interest of his mind"; and both Robert Graves and Anthony Burgess described him as the leading critic of his time. His exegesis of the *Sonnets* remains unsurpassed.
2001 • 194 pages • ISBN 978-1-871551-38-9

The Rain and the Glass *by Robert Nye*
When Robert Nye's first poems were published, G.S. Fraser declared in the *Times Literary Supplement*: "Here is a proper poet, though it is hard to see how the larger literary public (greedy for flattery of their own concerns) could be brought to recognize that. But other proper poets – how many of them are left? – will recognize one of themselves."
Since then Nye has become known to a large public for his novels, especially *Falstaff* (1976), winner of the Hawthornden Prize and The Guardian Fiction Prize, and *The Late Mr Shakespeare* (1998). But his true vocation has always been poetry, and it is as a poet that he is best known to his fellow poets. "Nye is the inheritor of a poetic tradition that runs from Donne and Ralegh

to Edward Thomas and Robert Graves," wrote James Aitchison in 1990, while the critic Gabriel Josipovici has described him as "one of the most interesting poets writing today, with a voice unlike that of any of his contemporaries".

This book contains all the poems Nye has written since his *Collected Poems* of 1995, together with his own selection from that volume. An introduction, telling the story of his poetic beginnings, affirms Nye's unfashionable belief in inspiration, as well as defining that quality of unforced truth which distinguishes the best of his work: "I have spent my life trying to write poems, but the poems gathered here came mostly when I was not."

2005 • 132 pages • ISBN 978-1-871551-41-9

Wilderness *by Martin Seymour-Smith*
This is Martin Seymour-Smith's first publication of his poetry for more than twenty years. This collection of 36 poems is a fearless account of an inner life of love, frustration, guilt, laughter and the celebration of others. He is best known to the general public as the author of the controversial and bestselling *Hardy* (1994).

1994 • 52 pages • ISBN 978-1-871551-08-2

STUDENT GUIDE LITERARY SERIES

The Greenwich Exchange Student Guide Literary Series is a collection of critical essays of major or contemporary serious writers in English and selected European languages. The series is for the student, the teacher and 'common readers' and is an ideal resource for libraries. The *Times Educational Supplement* praised these books, saying, "The style of [this series] has a pressure of meaning behind it. Readers should learn from that … If art is about selection, perception and taste, then this is it."

(ISBN prefix 978-1-871551- applies)
All books are paperbacks unless otherwise stated

The series includes:
W.H. Auden by Stephen Wade (36-5)
Honoré de Balzac by Wendy Mercer (48-8)
William Blake by Peter Davies (27-3)
The Brontës by Peter Davies (24-2)
Robert Browning by John Lucas (59-4)
Lord Byron by Andrew Keanie (83-9)
Samuel Taylor Coleridge by Andrew Keanie (64-8)
Joseph Conrad by Martin Seymour-Smith (18-1)